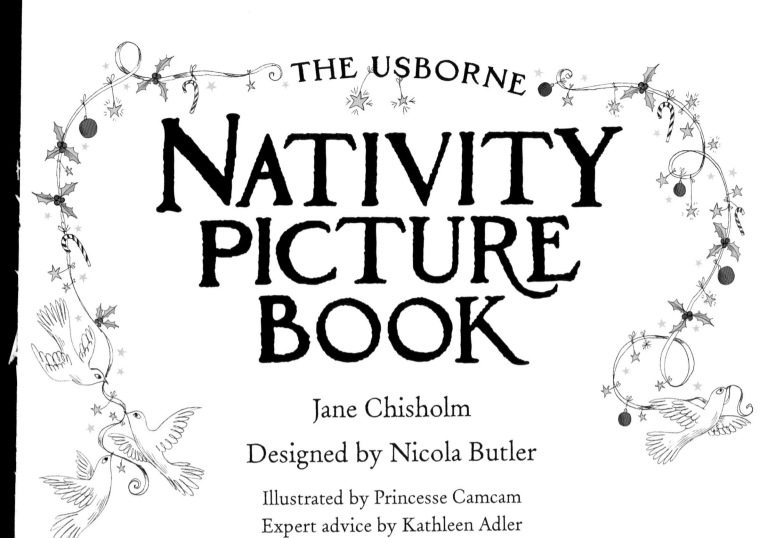

THE USBORNE
NATIVITY PICTURE BOOK

Jane Chisholm

Designed by Nicola Butler

Illustrated by Princesse Camcam
Expert advice by Kathleen Adler

CONTENTS

MARY AND THE ANGEL

Long, long ago, in a village called Nazareth, there lived a girl named Mary. One day, an angel flew down to her from Heaven and told her he had good news. "God has chosen you to have his baby son," said the angel.

This painting of Mary and the angel is covered in lots of real gold leaf. Notice the bright glow, or halo, around their heads. Many artists used these as a sign that someone was very holy.

The angel's name was Gabriel. He's carrying a branch of an olive tree – this is meant to show that he comes in peace.

THE ANNUNCIATION AND TWO SAINTS
1333
Simone Martini

Mary looks startled to see the angel, but the angel is reassuring her. The artist painted words coming out of Gabriel's mouth. They're in Latin, and they mean, 'Hail Mary, full of grace, God is with you.'

Ave Maria Gratia Plena Deus Tecum

THE ANNUNCIATION: THE ANGEL GABRIEL
Before 1511
Gaudenzio Ferrari

This painting of the angel Gabriel shows the same words on a scroll. Like lots of nativity paintings it was made as part of an altarpiece, to go inside a church.

Here, Mary is in her bedroom praying when she sees the angel. Can you spot the dove flying in above Gabriel's head? The bird was meant to symbolize the Holy Spirit.

THE ANNUNCIATION
About 1440-1445
Zanobi Strozzi

THE ANNUNCIATION
1307/8-11
Duccio

The scene on the left was originally part of a magnificent altarpiece made for Siena Cathedral in Italy – but it was later divided up into smaller paintings which you can see today in different museums all over the world.

Notice the vase of lilies at Mary's feet. They are meant to be a sign of Mary's purity.

The painting below of Mary and the angel was intended for a palace. It belonged to the wealthy Medici family in Florence, and may have been placed over a door, or been part of a piece of furniture.

The angel Gabriel is sometimes shown with peacock feather wings.

Look very closely at the stone carving. Can you spot three feathers inside a ring? This was an emblem of the Medici family.

THE ANNUNCIATION
About 1450-1453
Fra Filippo Lippi

3

TO BETHLEHEM

The months flew by and soon Mary's baby
was almost ready to be born. Then a message came
from the ruler of the land. Everyone had to go to their
family's home town to be counted. This was called the Census.

THE DREAM OF SAINT JOSEPH
1642-1643
Philippe de Champaigne

Mary was engaged to be married to a
carpenter named Joseph. Here, an
angel appears to him in a dream,
telling him that Mary would have a
baby who would be the son of God.

The artist painted
these tools to show
that Joseph was
a carpenter.

In the painting below, you can see Mary riding on a donkey with Joseph
walking beside her, as they set off for Bethlehem, Joseph's home town.

Bethlehem is a small town in
the Middle East, surrounded by
rocky desert and palm trees...

...but the artist of this painting had never
been there. So he made the landscape look green
and lush, like the Netherlands, where he lived.
The buildings look like European castles too.

THE ARRIVAL IN BETHLEHEM
About 1540
Attributed to Master LC

4

This painting of the Bethlehem Census – where Mary and Joseph went to be counted – is by another artist from the Netherlands.

It would never have snowed in Bethlehem, but he's set the scene in a busy village in winter – to make it real for the people in his country at the time.

Even though they're disguised in heavy winter clothing, you can still make out a woman on a donkey and a man with a saw. They're meant to be Mary and Joseph.

THE CENSUS IN BETHLEHEM
1566
Pieter Bruegel the Elder

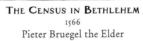

In the middle of the painting, there are villagers enjoying a snowball fight.

French artist Paul Gauguin set this snowy painting of Christmas Night in his native village of Pont-Aven in Brittany, France, just over 100 years ago. The women are wearing Breton costumes, and guiding their oxen towards a traditional Christmas crib.

CHRISTMAS NIGHT
1902-1903
Paul Gauguin

5

JESUS IS BORN

When Mary and Joseph arrived in Bethlehem,
it was nearly dark. They walked through the streets,
but couldn't find anywhere to stay. Finally, an innkeeper
offered them the stable, where he kept his animals. That night,
Mary gave birth to a baby boy, and she named him Jesus.

This night scene is so dark that you can barely see Joseph or the animals standing behind the manger. But the artist has painted a brilliant glow coming from the baby, lighting up the faces of Mary and the angels, emphasizing the wonder of the birth.

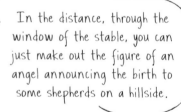

In the distance, through the window of the stable, you can just make out the figure of an angel announcing the birth to some shepherds on a hillside.

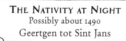

THE NATIVITY AT NIGHT
Possibly about 1490
Geertgen tot Sint Jans

The stable in this picture is made up of crumbling pillars – while in the distance you can see the church spires of a little town. The artist may have meant this as a symbol of the end of ancient Roman times and the arrival of Christianity.

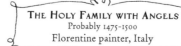

THE HOLY FAMILY WITH ANGELS
Probably 1475-1500
Florentine painter, Italy

The brilliant blue of Mary's dress comes from lapis lazuli, a semi-precious stone used to make the most expensive paint.

In the Middle Ages, roses were regarded as the 'queen of flowers' and were often used as a symbol for Mary.

The 19th century English artist Arthur Hughes has shown Mary wrapping her new baby in clothes. The straw on the floor and the crowded scene reminds us what a simple place Jesus was born in.

THE MADONNA OF THE ROSE GARDEN
About 1440-1442
Stephan Lochner

The rose garden is a symbol for paradise – a word that comes from the old Persian for 'enclosed garden'.

The idea of ornamental gardens was brought to Europe by crusader knights coming back from the Middle East.

THE NATIVITY
1857-1858
Arthur Hughes

THE MADONNA OF THE PINKS
About 1506-1507
Raphael

This painting is small enough to carry around in your hand. It focuses on the tender emotion between Mary, a young mother, and her child, Jesus.

Mary is often called the Madonna – meaning 'my lady' in Italian.

The tiny pink flowers are called pinks. They are meant to be a sign of love and marriage.

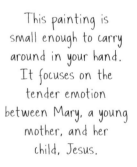

7

THE SHEPHERDS

Out on the hills at night, shepherds watching
over their sheep saw an angel in the sky. "Tonight the son
of God was born in a stable in Bethlehem," said the angel.
So the shepherds set off at once to visit him.

THE HOLY FAMILY WITH A SHEPHERD
About 1510
Titian

Here, one of the shepherds is
crouching down to look at the baby
Jesus. But, in the distance, you
can still make out an angel
fluttering among the trees,
announcing the birth to
the shepherds on the hills.

It wasn't unusual in paintings made at this
time to show two scenes happening at once.

In this painting, a small crowd has gathered to
celebrate Jesus's birth. Two shepherds, one of
them pointing up to heaven, are joined by five
angels singing, two of them playing lutes.

Even the animals seem to realize
something miraculous has happened.
Notice the donkey braying...

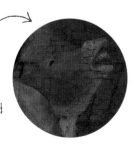

... and the magpie perched
silently on the roof.

THE NATIVITY
1470-1475
Piero della Francesca

Without the title, you might not realize this is a nativity scene. The artist Georges de la Tour painted the shepherds as if they were 17th century French peasants...

...but the deep glow from the candle shining around Jesus suggests that this is no ordinary baby.

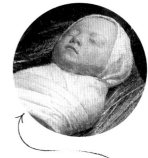

THE ADORATION OF THE SHEPHERDS
1645-1650
Georges de la Tour

A crowd of shepherds, young and old, flock to see the baby in the stable below. In the sky above, angels carry a banner with the words Gloria in Excelsis Deo – Latin for 'Glory be to God in the highest'.

Gloria in Excelsis Deo

Gloria in Excelsis Deo

The medieval painting on the right, of the shepherds with their flocks, was made as part of a book. Notice the mixture of black and white sheep and the sheepdog waiting patiently with his masters.

THE ADORATION OF THE SHEPHERDS
About 1640
Guido Reni

ANNUNCIATION TO THE SHEPHERDS
1411-1416
Limbourg brothers

9

THE STAR IN THE EAST

Far, far away in the East, three wise men
saw a bright star twinkling in the sky. "It's a sign that a new
king has been born," said one of them. So they followed
the star across the desert to Bethlehem.

The wise men are often known as magi, after priests of ancient Persia, who were famous for their skill at magic and interpreting the stars.

In this painting, the wise men's journey has become a grand procession – with birds and dogs and exotic animals, and nobles in sumptuous costumes.

It was commissioned by Cosimo de Medici, for the chapel in his palace in Florence, Italy. Many of the characters are based on members of his family.

THE JOURNEY OF THE MAGI TO BETHLEHEM
About 1460
Benozzo Gozzoli

The three wise men are often known as the three kings. One of the kings is shown here – experts believe it's a portrait of Cosimo's eleven-year-old grandson, Lorenzo.

The artist included himself in the painting, too. He is in the red hat, looking towards us.

In the distance, you can see a grand palace – probably the Medici Palace.

The artist of this painting has paid a lot of attention to animals –
horses of different shades, dogs running alongside, a couple of cranes in
the top left-hand corner and a monkey being brought as an exotic gift.
One of the horses has even been painted from behind.

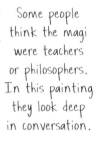

Some people
think the magi
were teachers
or philosophers.
In this painting
they look deep
in conversation.

There are lots of stories about
where the magi came from. Some
believe it was Persia. Others
suggest Arabia or Ethiopia. But
each one may have come from a
different place.

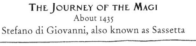

THE JOURNEY OF THE MAGI
About 1435
Stefano di Giovanni, also known as Sassetta

This 14th-century map shows the
magi riding to Bethlehem from
Tarssia in Central Asia. As well
as characters from the Bible, it
includes exotic places European
explorers had recently discovered.

Notice the ceremonial elephant
in the kingdom of the Sultan
of Delhi and a Chinese boat,
called a junk, sailing off the
west coast of India.

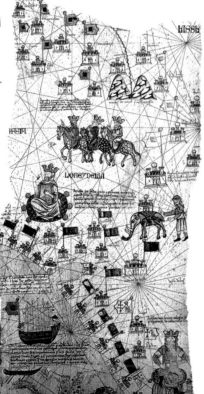

Among the oldest surviving images
of the three wise men is this mosaic, made
1,500 years ago for a church in Ravenna,
Italy. You can see their names above the
figures – Balthazar, Melchior and Caspar.

**THE THREE MAGI FROM THE PROVINCE OF
TARSSIA FROM THE CATALAN ATLAS**
1375
Abraham Cresques

THREE MAGI
From about 560
From the Basilica
of Sant'Appollinare Nuovo,
Ravenna, Italy

THE THREE KINGS

The three kings journeyed across the desert
by night, following the star, until it stopped above the
stable in Bethlehem. When they saw the newborn baby Jesus,
they gave him gifts of gold, frankincense and myrrh.

Frankincense and myrrh
were incense from the resin of
trees which grew in Arabia and
North Africa. The incense was so
highly valued that at one point
myrrh was as expensive as gold.

A myrrh tree

Notice the star shining
over the stable roof.

This stained glass picture of the
three kings presenting gifts was
made just over a hundred years
ago, for the window of a church.

THE ADORATION OF THE KINGS
1510-1515
Jan Gossaert

The kings are all richly dressed and each has brought
their own servants with them. One of them is presenting
Mary with another gift – gold coins in a chalice.

This scene,
painted on
wood, was
probably part
of an altarpiece
in a church.

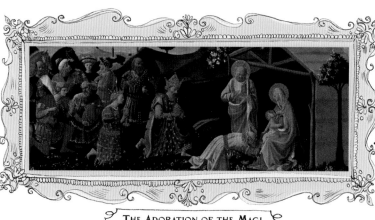

THE ADORATION
OF THE KINGS
1879
Edward Burne-Jones
and William Morris

THE ADORATION OF THE MAGI
1433-1434
Attributed to Zanobi Strozzi

Here, one of the kings
has handed his gift to Joseph
and is kissing the baby's foot.

12

The artist of this painting has set the nativity in a village in his own country – the Netherlands – in midwinter. Half the village seems to have turned up with the kings and the shepherds.

There are lots of tiny details of village life – notice the woman with a baby chatting with a man on a horse.

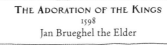

THE ADORATION OF THE KINGS
1598
Jan Brueghel the Elder

If you look closely, can you see Joseph's carpentry tools in the bottom right-hand corner...

... and skaters on the lake in the distance?

Everyone in this magnificent painting of the three kings is dressed in rich Renaissance costumes, decorated with embroidered patterns.

The painting is decorated in real gold and there are precious stones embedded in the panels.

THE ADORATION OF THE MAGI
1423
Gentile da Fabriano

Apart from horses and dogs, the artist has added all sorts of animals. Can you spot a lion, an Arabian camel, some apes...

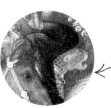

... and a leopard?

This lower panel shows other scenes from the story.

1

THE ANNUNCIATION
1307/8-11
Duccio

One day, the angel Gabriel flew down to Mary and told her she would soon have a baby boy, and he would be the son of God.

THE NATIVITY AT NIGHT
Possibly about 1490
Geertgen tot Sint Jans

Mary and Joseph set off for Bethlehem. There, they were given shelter in a stable, where Mary gave birth to baby Jesus.

2

3

THE HOLY FAMILY WITH A SHEPHERD
About 1510
Titian

An angel spoke to nearby shepherds, watching their sheep, telling them that Jesus was born. They went to visit him in the stable.

4

THE ADORATION OF THE KINGS
1598
Jan Brueghel the Elder

Far away, three kings followed a bright star all the way to visit Jesus, too. They brought him gifts of gold, frankincense and myrrh.

THE NATIVITY STORY

USBORNE QUICKLINKS

For links to websites where you can examine many of the paintings in this book close up and find out more about them, go to the Usborne Quicklinks website at **www.usborne.com/quicklinks** and enter the keywords **"Nativity picture book"**. Please follow the internet safety guidelines at the Quicklinks website.

Usborne Publishing is not responsible and does not accept liability for the availability or content of any website other than its own, or for any exposure to harmful, offensive, or inaccurate material which may appear on the Web or any damage or loss caused by viruses that may be downloaded as a result of browsing the sites it recommends.

ACKNOWLEDGEMENTS

Cover *Madonna of the Pinks* by Raphael (National Gallery, London) © The National Gallery, London. *The Adoration of the Magi* attributed to Zanobi Strozzi (National Gallery, London) © The National Gallery, London. *The Annunciation* by Zanobi Strozzi (National Gallery, London) © The National Gallery, London. **Page 2:** *The Annunciation and Two Saints* by Simone Martini, complete work and detail (Galleria degli Uffizi, Florence) © 2011. Photo Scala, Florence - courtesy of the Ministero Beni e Att. Culturali. *The Annunciation: The Angel Gabriel* by Gaudenzio Ferrari (National Gallery, London) © The National Gallery, London. **Page 3:** *The Annunciation* by Zanobi Strozzi, see cover for credit © The National Gallery, London. *The Annunciation* by Duccio (National Gallery, London) © The National Gallery, London. *The Annunciation* by Fra Filippo Lippi, complete work and detail (National Gallery, London) © The National Gallery, London. **Page 4:** *The Dream of Saint Joseph* by Philippe de Champaigne, complete work and detail (National Gallery, London) © The National Gallery, London. *The Arrival in Bethlehem*, attributed to Master LC (Metropolitan Museum of Art, New York) © 2011. Image copyright The Metropolitan Museum of Art/Art Resource/Scala, Florence. **Page 5:** *The Census in Bethlehem* by Pieter Bruegel the Elder, complete work and details (Musées Royaux des Beaux-Arts, Brussels) © 2011. Photo Scala, Florence. *Christmas Night* by Paul Gauguin (Indianapolis Museum of Art, USA) © Indianapolis Museum of Art, USA/The Bridgeman Art Library. **Page 6:** *The Nativity at Night* by Geertgen tot Sint Jans, complete work and detail (National Gallery, London) © The National Gallery, London. *The Holy Family with Angels* by a Florentine painter, complete work and detail (National Gallery, London) © The National Gallery, London. **Page 7:** *The Madonna of the Rose Garden* by Stephan Lochner, complete work and detail (Wallraf Richartz Museum, Cologne, Germany) © Giraudon/The Bridgeman Art Library. *The Nativity* by Arthur Hughes (Birmingham Museums and Art Gallery, UK) © Birmingham Museums and Art Gallery/The Bridgeman Art Library. *The Madonna of the Pinks* by Raphael, see credit for cover. **Page 8:** *The Holy Family with a Shepherd* by Titian, complete work and detail (National Gallery, London) © The National Gallery, London. *The Nativity* by Piero della Francesca, complete work and details (National Gallery, London) © The National Gallery, London. **Page 9:** *The Adoration of the Shepherds* by Georges de La Tour, complete work and detail (Louvre, Paris) © 2011. Photo Scala, Florence. *The Adoration of the Shepherds* by Guido Reni (National Gallery, London) © The National Gallery, London. *Annunciation to the Shepherds* by the Limbourg brothers (Musée Condé, Chantilly, France) © RMN, Les Très Riches Heures du Duc de Berry, Les heures de la vierge: l'annonce aux bergers, Ms65-folio48recto/René-Gabriel Ojéda. **Page 10:** *The Journey of the Magi to Bethlehem* by Benozzo Gozzoli, complete work and details (Palazzo Medici-Riccardi, Florence, Italy) © The Bridgeman Art Library. **Page 11:** *The Journey of the Magi* by Stefano di Giovanni, also known as Sasseta, complete work and detail (Metropolitan Museum of Art, New York, USA) © Metropolitan Museum of Art, New York, USA/The Bridgeman Art Library. *Three Magi from the Catalan Atlas* 1375 by Abraham Cresques (Bibliothèque Nationale, Paris) © 2011. White Images/Scala, Florence. *Three Magi from the Basilica of Sant'Appollinare Nuovo*, Ravenna, Italy © 2011. Photo Scala, Florence - courtesy of the Ministero Beni e Att. Culturali. **Page 12:** *The Adoration of the Kings* by Jan Gossaert, complete work and detail (National Gallery, London) © The National Gallery, London. *The Adoration of the Kings* by Edward Burne-Jones and William Morris (All Saints Church, Sheepy Magna, Leicestershire, UK) © Colin Underhill/Alamy. *The Adoration of the Magi* attributed to Zanobi Strozzi, see credit for cover. **Page 13:** *The Adoration of the Kings* by Jan Brueghel the Elder, complete work and detail (National Gallery, London) © The National Gallery, London. *The Adoration of the Magi* by Gentile da Fabriano, complete work and details (Galleria degli Uffizi, Florence, Italy) © Galleria degli Uffizi, Florence, Italy/The Bridgeman Art Library. **Page 14:** *The Annunciation* by Duccio (National Gallery, London) © The National Gallery, London. *The Nativity at Night* by Geertgen tot Sint Jans, complete work and detail (National Gallery, London) © The National Gallery, London. **Page 15:** *The Holy Family with a Shepherd* by Titian, complete work and detail (National Gallery, London) © The National Gallery, London. *The Adoration of the Kings* by Jan Gossaert, complete work and detail (National Gallery, London) © The National Gallery, London.

INDEX